The Divine Path to Motherhood

Orange Books Publication

1st Floor, Rajhans Arcade, Mall Road, Kohka, Bhilai, Chhattisgarh 490020
Website: **www.orangebooks.in**

© Copyright, 2024, Author

All rights reserved. No part of this book may be reproduced, stored in a retrieval system, or transmitted, in any form by any means, electronic, mechanical, magnetic, optical, chemical, manual, photocopying, recording or otherwise, without the prior written consent of its writer.

First Edition, 2024

ISBN: 978-93-6554-325-4

The Divine Path to
MOTHERHOOD

SEVEN SPIRITUAL LAWS FOR A BLISSFUL PREGNANCY

DR MEHUL KIRITKUMAR NAYAK

Orange Books Publication
www.orangebooks.in

Disclaimer

Important Notice:

The content presented in this book, *"The Divine Path to Motherhood: Seven Spiritual Laws for a Blissful Pregnancy"* is intended for informational and inspirational purposes only. While the principles and practices outlined in this book are designed to support expecting mothers on their spiritual journey through pregnancy, they are not a substitute for professional medical advice, diagnosis, or treatment.

Consult with Healthcare Professionals: Always seek the guidance of your healthcare provider with any questions you may have regarding your pregnancy, medical conditions, or treatments. Do not disregard professional medical advice or delay seeking it because of information you have read in this book.

Individual Variations: Every pregnancy is unique. The suggestions and practices described in this book may not be suitable for all individuals. It is essential to consider your specific health circumstances and to consult with your healthcare provider before adopting any new practices or making significant changes to your lifestyle during pregnancy.

No Guarantees: The author and publisher make no guarantees or warranties, expressed or implied, about the completeness, accuracy, reliability, suitability, or availability of the information contained in this book. The application of the Seven Spiritual Laws and their outcomes may vary for each individual.

Limitation of Liability: The author and publisher disclaim any liability for any physical, emotional, or psychological harm, injury, or damage that may result from the use or misuse of the information provided in this book. Readers assume full responsibility for their choices and actions.

By using this book, you acknowledge and agree to this disclaimer. Your journey through pregnancy is deeply personal, and it is important to prioritize your health and well-being, guided by the advice and support of qualified healthcare professionals.

With warm wishes for a healthy and joyful pregnancy.

[DR MEHUL KIRITKUMAR NAYAK]

"The Divine Path to Motherhood: Seven Spiritual Laws for a Blissful Pregnancy"

Acknowledgment

This book, "The Divine Path to Motherhood: Seven Spiritual Laws for a Blissful Pregnancy," is the culmination of a journey that would not have been possible without the support, guidance, and inspiration of many wonderful individuals.

First and foremost, I express my deepest gratitude to my family. Your unwavering love and encouragement have been the foundation of my work. To my parents, thank you for your blessings and for instilling in me the values, that have guided me throughout my life. To my loving spouse, your patience and understanding have been my rock, allowing me to pursue my passion for writing this book. To my children, your smiles and innocence remind me of the beauty of life and the miracle of motherhood.

I am immensely grateful to my colleagues and friends at Krishna Hospital, Tharad. Your professional insights and camaraderie have enriched my understanding and approach to the spiritual aspects of pregnancy. A special thanks to Dr. Ravindrabhai Chaudhary, Dr. Karsanbhai R. Patel, Dr. Jaydipbhai Chaudhary, Dr. Jayeshbhai Chaudhary, Dr. Kantibhai Manvar and Dr Tejasbhai Barot for your support and contributions. A special thanks to Mr. Kunal Mevada for unwavering love and encouragement. My heartfelt appreciation goes to all the mothers who shared their stories and experiences with me. Your courage and resilience are truly inspiring, and your insights have added depth and authenticity to this book.

A special note of gratitude goes to Hemrajbhai for your meticulous grammar corrections. Your attention to detail has significantly improved the clarity and readability of this work.

I am deeply indebted to Dr. Deepak Chopra. Sir, your original, world-best-selling book, "The Seven Spiritual Laws of Success," has been a profound source of inspiration for me. Your wisdom and teachings have greatly influenced the seven laws for joyful pregnancy presented in this book.

Lastly, I extend my gratitude to the readers of this book. It is my sincere hope that "The Divine Path to Motherhood: Seven Spiritual Laws for blissful Pregnancy" serves as a source of inspiration, comfort, and joy during this extraordinary phase of your life.

With deepest thanks and blessings,

Dr. Mehul Kiritkumar Nayak

Introduction

The Journey of Pregnancy

Welcome to "The Seven Spiritual Laws of Success in Pregnancy," a guide crafted to support you through one of the most transformative journeys of your life.

Pregnancy is not just a physical process; it is a profound spiritual experience that invites you to connect deeply with your inner self, your growing baby, and the universe around you.

Embracing the Journey

Pregnancy is a time of incredible change, growth, and new beginnings. As you prepare to bring new life into the world, you are also embarking on a journey of personal and spiritual development. This book aims to provide you with the wisdom and tools to navigate this journey with grace, peace, and joy.

Understanding the Seven Spiritual Laws

The Seven Spiritual Laws of Success, originally articulated by Deepak Chopra, are universal principles that can be applied to all aspects of life. In this book, we will explore how these laws can specifically guide you through pregnancy, helping you to nurture your body, mind, and spirit.

1. **The Law of Pure Potentiality:** Recognize and embrace your limitless potential as a mother. Connect with your inner self and the infinite possibilities that lie ahead.

2. **The Law of Giving:** Learn the power of giving and receiving love, care, and kindness. Discover how nurturing yourself positively impacts your baby.
3. **The Law of Karma:** Understand the importance of conscious choices and their effects. Cultivate positive actions and intentions for a harmonious pregnancy.
4. **The Law of Least Effort:** Embrace the natural flow of pregnancy. Learn to let go of stress and allow your body and mind to relax and adapt.
5. **The Law of Intention and Desire:** Set clear and positive intentions for your pregnancy and birth. Visualize and manifest a healthy and joyful journey.
6. **The Law of Detachment:** Release fears and uncertainties. Trust the natural process of pregnancy and remain flexible and adaptable.
7. **The Law of Dharma:** Discover the sacred role of motherhood. Find meaning and fulfillment in your journey and connect with your life's purpose as a mother.

Preparing for Transformation

Each chapter of this book will delve into one of the seven laws, offering practical exercises, meditations, and reflections to help you integrate these principles into your daily life. By embracing these spiritual laws, you will not only enhance your pregnancy experience but also prepare yourself for the beautiful transition into motherhood.

A Journey of Love and Connection

Pregnancy is a unique opportunity to deepen your connection with yourself, your baby, and the world around you. It is a journey of love, growth, and spiritual awakening. As you read through this book, allow yourself to be open to the wisdom and guidance it offers. Trust that you have all the resources within you to create a fulfilling and joyful pregnancy.

Welcome to this journey of transformation. May you find peace, joy, and spiritual fulfillment as you prepare to welcome your new baby into the world.

Contents

Chapter 1
The Law of Pure Potentiality 1
Connecting With Your Inner Self.............................. 1
Meditation And Mindfulness Practices For Expecting Mothers.. 2
Embracing Silence And Self-Reflection 3

Chapter 2
The Law of Giving For Pregnant Mothers................... 5
Nurturing Yourself And Your Baby 5
Acts Of Kindness And Generosity 6
Sharing Love And Positive Energy 7

Chapter 3
The Law of Karma (Cause And Effect) 10
Actions And Reactions During Pregnancy 10
Making Conscious Choices 11
Cultivating Positive Intentions.......................................11

Chapter4
The Law of Least Effort 15
Letting Go Of Stress And Strain......................................15
Accepting And Flowing With Changes 16
Practicing Relaxation And Gentle Movement 17

Chapter 5

The Law of Intention And Desire 21
Setting Positive Intentions For Your Pregnancy And Birth 21
Visualizing A Healthy And A Joyful Journey...................22

Chapter 6

The Law of Detachment 26
Releasing Fear And Uncertainty....................................26
Trusting The Natural Process Of Pregnancy..................27
Embracing Flexibility And Adaptability 28

Chapter 7

The Law of Dharma (Purpose In Life) 30
Recognizing The Sacred Role Of Motherhood...............30
Finding Meaning And Fulfillment In Pregnancy 31
Connecting With Your Life's Purpose As A Mother 31

Chapter 8

PRACTICAL APPLICATIONS OF THE SEVEN SPIRITUAL LAWS OF SUCCESS DURING PREGNANCY... 34
Daily Practices To Integrate The Seven Laws 34
Creating A Supportive Environment..............................37
Building A Community Of Love And Support.................37

Conclusion

Reflecting On Your Journey 39
Preparing For The Transition To Motherhood...............39
Embracing The Future With Confidence And Joy 40

Chapter 1

The Law of Pure Potentiality

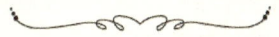

Connecting with Your Inner Self

Introduction

Every expecting mother embarks on a transformative journey that goes beyond the physical changes. It's a time of profound spiritual growth and self-discovery. The Law of Pure Potentiality is about recognizing the infinite possibilities within you. It's about tapping into the core of your being, where pure consciousness resides, and realizing your true potential as a creator of your life.

Connecting with Your Inner Self

During pregnancy, your connection with your inner self deepens. This connection is the essence of the Law of Pure Potentiality. To access this inner realm, you must turn inward, away from the distractions of the external world.

Story: The Blossoming Lotus

Consider the story of Aarti, a mother-to-be, who discovered the power of connecting with her inner self. During her second trimester, Aarti felt overwhelmed by the changes and responsibilities that lay ahead. Her anxiety grew until she attended a prenatal yoga class, that introduced her to meditation and mindfulness. Through regular practice, Aarti found a peaceful space within herself, much like a lotus blooming in a serene pond. This inner sanctuary helped her navigate her pregnancy with grace and confidence.

Meditation and Mindfulness Practices for Expecting Mothers

Meditation is a powerful tool to connect with your inner self. It calms the mind, reduces stress, and fosters a deep sense of peace. For expecting mothers, meditation can enhance the bond with your unborn child and provide emotional stability.

Guided Meditation: The Heartbeat Connection

1. **Find a Quiet Space:** Sit comfortably in a quiet room, free from distractions.
2. **Focus on Your Breath:** Close your eyes and take deep, slow breaths. Inhale through your nose, filling your lungs, and exhale through your mouth.
3. **Visualize Your Baby:** As you continue to breathe, visualize your baby growing inside you. Feel the connection between your breath and your baby's heartbeat.
4. **Repeat a Mantra:** Silently repeat a calming mantra, such as "I am calm, I am connected." Allow this mantra to guide you into a state of deep relaxation.
5. **Embrace the Silence:** Sit in this peaceful state for 10-15 minutes, focusing on the bond between you and your baby.

Example: Mindful Walking

Another effective mindfulness practice is mindful walking. Take a slow, deliberate walk in nature. Pay attention to each step, the sensation of your feet touching the ground, the sounds around you, and the rhythm of your breath. This practice helps ground you in the present moment and enhances your connection with your inner self and your baby.

Embracing Silence and Self-Reflection

Silence is a powerful ally in accessing pure potentiality. In the silence, you can hear the whispers of your soul and the wisdom of your body.

"In the silence of our hearts, we find the guidance of our souls". Deepak Chopra

Story: The Silent Retreat

Meera, another expectant mother, found solace in silence. She attended a silent retreat designed for pregnant women. The retreat offered a space free from the noise of daily life, allowing Meera to focus inward. In this silence, she reflected on her journey, her hopes for her child, and her dreams as a mother. This experience not only deepened her spiritual connection but also gave her clarity and strength.

Self-Reflection Practices

1. Journaling: Spend a few minutes each day writing down your thoughts and feelings. Reflect on your journey, your aspirations, and your experiences. Journaling can be a powerful tool for self-discovery and emotional release.

2. Affirmations: Create positive affirmations that resonate with your goals and dreams as a mother. Repeat these affirmations daily to reinforce a positive mindset.

3. Visualization: Visualize your ideal birth experience and the kind of mother you want to be. Picture yourself holding your healthy, happy baby. This positive visualization can help manifest your desires.

Conclusion

The Law of Pure Potentiality reminds us that we are not limited by our circumstances. As an expecting mother, you hold within yourself the potential to create a beautiful, fulfilling journey for yourself and your child. By connecting with your inner self, practicing meditation and mindfulness, embracing silence and self-reflection, you can unlock this potential and navigate your pregnancy with peace, joy, and confidence.

Chapter 2

The Law of Giving for Pregnant Mothers

Nurturing Yourself and Your Baby

Pregnancy is a transformative journey that involves physical, emotional, and spiritual changes. The Law of Giving, one of the Seven Spiritual Laws of Success, emphasizes the importance of giving and receiving, which plays a crucial role in nurturing yourself and your baby.

Giving during pregnancy can start with self-care. Nurturing yourself with proper nutrition, rest, and relaxation directly benefits your baby. For example, eating a balanced diet rich in vitamins and minerals supports your baby's growth and development.

Incorporating mindfulness practices such as meditation and yoga can reduce stress, promoting a calm and healthy environment for your baby.

A touching story is that of Maya, a pregnant mother who started her mornings with a gratitude journal. Every day, she wrote down three things she was grateful for and three acts of kindness she planned to perform. This practice not only uplifted her spirit but also fostered a positive and nurturing environment for her baby.

"The best way to find yourself is to lose yourself in the service of others." — Mahatma Gandhi

Acts of Kindness and Generosity

Acts of kindness and generosity are powerful expressions of the Law of Giving. These acts create a ripple effect, benefiting both the giver and the receiver. During pregnancy, engaging in acts of kindness can enhance your emotional well-being and strengthen your bond with your baby.

Consider the story of Anjali, who volunteered at a local community center during her pregnancy. She spent her afternoons reading to children, sharing stories of hope and kindness. This act of giving not only brought joy to the children but also filled Anjali with a sense of purpose and connection.

Giving can also take the form of small, everyday gestures. Smiling at a stranger, offering a kind word, or helping a neighbor with groceries are simple yet profound ways to practice generosity. These acts of kindness contribute to a positive atmosphere, benefiting everyone involved.

In the journey of life, each human being is blessed with five invaluable diamonds that illuminate the path of giving. The first diamond is our face, a canvas for smiles that brighten the world around us. The second diamond, our eyes, reveals love and deep feelings, creating connections that transcend words. The third diamond, our lips, has the power to uplift others with courageous and positive words. The fourth diamond is our heart, a wellspring of goodwill and prayers for others, radiating compassion and kindness. Lastly, the fifth diamond is our body, through which we can serve our community, support other mothers, and care for ourselves. By embracing these gifts, we fulfill the profound spiritual law of giving, enriching our lives and of those we touch.

"We make a living by what we get. We make a life by what we give." — Winston Churchill

Sharing Love and Positive Energy

Sharing love and positive energy is at the heart of the Law of Giving. Love is a powerful force that can transform lives and create lasting bonds. During pregnancy, sharing love with your partner, family, and community can create a supportive and nurturing environment for your baby.

The story of Priya and Rahul illustrates the power of love and positive energy. Throughout Priya's pregnancy, Rahul made it a point to express his love and appreciation for her daily. He left sweet notes around the house, cooked her favorite meals, and spent quality time talking and listening to her. This constant flow of love and positive energy not only strengthened their relationship but also created a warm and loving atmosphere for their baby.

Positive energy can also be shared through words and actions. Complimenting someone, expressing gratitude, or offering encouragement are ways to spread positivity. These actions not only uplift others but also reflect back, creating a cycle of positive energy.

"Love and compassion are necessities, not luxuries. Without them, humanity cannot survive." — Dalai Lama

The Impact of Giving on Mother and Baby

The act of giving has profound effects on both the mother and the baby. When a pregnant mother engages in giving, whether through self-care, acts of kindness, or sharing love, it promotes a sense of fulfillment and happiness. This positive emotional state is beneficial for the baby, as it creates a harmonious environment for growth and development.

Scientific studies have shown that maternal stress can negatively impact fetal development, whereas positive emotions and a supportive environment contribute to better outcomes for the baby. By practicing the Law of Giving, mothers can create a nurturing and positive atmosphere that supports the well-being of their baby.

For instance, Rina, who practiced giving by participating in community gardening, reported feeling more connected and content. She noticed that her stress levels decreased, and she felt more energized and positive. This, in turn, benefited her baby, as she experienced a smoother and more joyful pregnancy.

> *"The simplest acts of kindness are by far more powerful than a thousand heads bowing in prayer." — Mahatma Gandhi*

Practical Ways to Practice the Law of Giving During Pregnancy

To incorporate the Law of Giving into your daily life during pregnancy, consider these practical tips:

1. Self-Care Routine: Dedicate some time each day to nurture yourself. This can include healthy eating, regular exercise, meditation, or a relaxing bath.

2. Random Acts of Kindness: Perform small acts of kindness daily. This could be as simple as holding the door open for someone or leaving an uplifting note for a coworker.

3. Volunteer Work: Get involved in your community through volunteer work. This not only helps others but also provides a sense of purpose and connection.

4. Express Love: Regularly express your love and appreciation to your partner, family, and friends. Small gestures like saying "I love you" or giving a hug can make a big difference.

5. Positive Affirmations: Start your day with positive affirmations. This can set a positive tone for the day and help you stay focused on giving and receiving love and kindness.

By embracing the Law of Giving during pregnancy, you create a nurturing and positive environment that benefits both you and your baby. This chapter highlights the transformative power of giving and how it can enrich your pregnancy journey, fostering a deeper connection with yourself, your baby, and those around you.

Chapter 3

The Law of Karma (Cause and Effect)

Introduction: Understanding the Law of Karma

Karma, a Sanskrit term meaning "action" or "deed," is the spiritual principle of cause and effect. Essentially,

every action we take, whether good or bad, has consequences that will return to us in the future. This law is particularly relevant during pregnancy, a period of profound change and growth. Understanding and applying the law of karma can help expecting mothers cultivate a positive environment for their developing baby.

Actions and Reactions During Pregnancy

Every thought, word, and action has a ripple effect, influencing both the mother and her unborn child. Scientific studies have shown that a mother's emotional and mental state can significantly impact the baby's development. For example, stress and anxiety can lead to hormonal imbalances, affecting the baby's growth and health.

Example:

Anita, a 28-year-old pregnant woman, constantly worried about her job security. Her stress levels were high, leading to insomnia and a poor appetite. Her baby was born underweight and with a weak immune system. Conversely, her friend Priya, who practiced meditation and positive thinking throughout her pregnancy, gave birth to a healthy and happy baby.

"The energy you project is the energy you receive. During pregnancy, ensure your actions are filled with love and positivity, for they will shape the future of your child." — Unknown

Making Conscious Choices

Pregnancy is a time to make mindful choices that promote the well-being of both the mother and the baby. Conscious decision-making involves being aware of the consequences of our actions and choosing those that bring positive outcomes. This can range from dietary choices to emotional responses and lifestyle changes.

Story:

Meera, a pregnant mother, decided to switch to a healthier diet rich in fruits, vegetables, and whole grains. She also joined a prenatal yoga class to maintain her physical and mental health. By making these conscious choices, Meera not only felt more energetic and positive during her pregnancy but also gave birth to a robust and healthy baby.

"Our lives are shaped by our choices. During pregnancy, choose actions that nurture and uplift, for they create the foundation for your child's future." — Deepak Chopra

Cultivating Positive Intentions

Positive intentions are the seeds of positive actions. By fostering a mindset of love, gratitude, and compassion, pregnant mothers can create a nurturing environment for their babies. Positive intentions can be cultivated through practices such as meditation, affirmations, and gratitude journaling.

Example:

Rina, who was expecting her first child, started each day with a gratitude journal, writing down three things she was thankful for. She also practiced loving-kindness meditation, sending positive energy to her baby. Her positive intentions created a calm and joyful atmosphere, benefiting both her and her unborn child.

> *"Intention is the core of all conscious life. Your intention during pregnancy shapes the energy and experiences of both you and your baby."* — Gary Zukav

Real-Life Stories of Karma During Pregnancy

Story 1:

Sunita, a mother of two, shared her experience of how her kindness and generosity during her first pregnancy returned to her manifold during her second. During her first pregnancy, she volunteered at a local shelter, helping other expectant mothers in need. Years later, when she faced complications during her second pregnancy, she received overwhelming support from the community she had once helped.

Story 2:

Jyoti, a yoga instructor, shared how practicing and teaching prenatal yoga not only kept her fit but also positively influenced her baby. Her calm and composed demeanor, a result of her yoga practice, was mirrored in her baby's calm nature.

Practical Tips for Pregnant Mothers

1. Mindful Eating:

Choose nutritious foods that nourish both you and your baby. Avoid processed and junk foods that can lead to health issues.

2. Positive Thinking:
Practice daily affirmations to maintain a positive outlook. Surround yourself with positive people and environments.

3. Stress Management:
Engage in relaxation techniques such as meditation, deep breathing, or prenatal yoga.

Avoid stressful situations and seek support when needed.

4. Acts of Kindness:
Volunteer or help others in need, fostering a sense of community and goodwill.

Perform small acts of kindness, like sending thank-you notes or helping a neighbor.

5. Gratitude Practice:
Keep a gratitude journal to focus on the positive aspects of your life.

Express gratitude to those who support you during your pregnancy.

"By making mindful choices and cultivating positive intentions during pregnancy, you not only enhance your own well-being but also lay a strong foundation for your child's future." — Unknown

Conclusion: Embracing the Law of Karma

The law of karma teaches us that our actions have consequences, and by making conscious, positive choices, we can create a better future for ourselves and our children. During pregnancy, this principle is especially powerful. By understanding and applying the law of karma, expecting mothers can foster a nurturing environment that benefits both their well-being and the development of their unborn child. Embrace this journey with love, mindfulness, and positivity, knowing that every action you take, shapes the beautiful life growing within you.

Chapter 4

The Law of Least Effort

Introduction

Pregnancy is a transformative journey, filled with physical, emotional, and spiritual changes. During this period, embracing the Law of Least Effort can help expectant mothers navigate their experiences with grace and ease. This chapter explores how letting go of stress and strain, accepting and flowing with changes, and practicing relaxation and gentle movement can create a harmonious environment for both mother and baby.

Letting Go of Stress and Strain

One of the fundamental principles of the Law of Least Effort is the ability to release stress and strain. Pregnancy often brings about worries and anxieties, whether it's about the baby's health, the birth process, or the adjustments that will follow. By letting go of these stresses, mothers can foster a more peaceful state of mind, beneficial for both themselves and their babies.

Story: The Peaceful Journey of Maya

Maya was in her second trimester when she realized the constant worry about her baby's health was taking a toll on her well-being. Her doctor suggested incorporating daily meditation into her routine. Maya started practicing guided meditations that focused on breathing and visualizing a calm, safe environment for her baby. Over time, she noticed a significant decrease in her anxiety levels. The practice not only helped her relax but also strengthened her connection with her unborn child.

> *"Stress is not what happens to us. It's our response to what happens. And response is something we can choose." – Maureen Killoran*

Practical Tips:

Meditation: Dedicate a few minutes each day to meditate, focusing on your breath and the positive journey ahead.

Positive Affirmations: Use affirmations such as "I am calm and peaceful" or "My baby and I are healthy and safe" to counteract negative thoughts.

Mindfulness Practices: Engage in activities that bring you into the present moment, such as gentle walking or mindful eating.

Accepting and Flowing with Changes

Pregnancy is synonymous with change, from physical transformations to shifting emotions. Accepting and flowing with these changes rather than resisting them can lead to a more harmonious experience. The Law of Least Effort encourages us to embrace change as a natural part of life.

Story: Sara's Embrace of Change

Sara struggled with the rapid changes in her body during pregnancy. She often felt frustrated and disconnected. Her midwife introduced her to the concept of mindfulness, encouraging her to tune into her body and appreciate the incredible work it was doing. By practicing mindful body scans and attending prenatal yoga classes, Sara learned to accept and even celebrate the changes she was experiencing.

"Change is not something that we should fear. Rather, it is something that we should welcome. For without change, nothing in this world would ever grow or blossom." – B.K.S. Iyengar

Practical Tips:

Mindful Body Scans: Regularly practice body scans to become aware of your physical sensations without judgment.

Prenatal Yoga: Engage in prenatal yoga to connect with your changing body and prepare it for childbirth.

Journaling: Keep a pregnancy journal to reflect on your experiences and the positive aspects of change.

Practicing Relaxation and Gentle Movement

Incorporating relaxation techniques and gentle movements into your daily routine can significantly enhance your well-being during pregnancy. The Law of Least Effort emphasizes doing less and achieving more by aligning with nature's flow, which can be applied through activities that promote relaxation and gentle exercise.

Story: Emma's Journey with Gentle Movement

Emma found herself constantly exhausted during her pregnancy, struggling to keep up with her usual fitness routine. Her doctor recommended she try Tai Chi, a form of gentle movement that promotes relaxation and balance. Emma began practicing Tai Chi and soon found it not only invigorated her but also provided a sense of calm and clarity. It became her sanctuary, a time to connect with her baby and her body in a peaceful way.

"Nature does not hurry, yet everything is accomplished." – Lao Tzu

Practical Tips:

Tai Chi or Qi Gong: Explore these gentle forms of movement that focus on slow, deliberate motions and deep breathing.

Tai Chi is a traditional Chinese martial art known for its gentle, flowing movements and is often practiced for its health benefits. It is a form of exercise that combines deep breathing and relaxation with slow, deliberate movements. Here are key aspects of Tai Chi in movement and exercise:

Characteristics of Tai Chi Movements:

1. *Slow and Gentle*: The movements in Tai Chi are slow, smooth, and continuous, designed to improve flexibility, balance, and overall physical coordination.

2. *Focused Breathing*: Practitioners focus on deep, controlled breathing, which helps to relax the body and mind.

3. *Mindfulness*: Tai Chi incorporates elements of mindfulness and meditation, promoting a calm, focused mental state.

4. *Balance and Coordination*: The movements emphasize weight transfer and balance, enhancing stability and reducing the risk of falls.

Health Benefits of Tai Chi:

1. *Improves Balance and Reduces Falls*: Especially beneficial for older adults, helping to enhance proprioception and coordination.

2. *Enhances Flexibility and Strength*: Regular practice can increase muscle strength, flexibility, and joint mobility.

3. *Reduces Stress and Anxiety*: The meditative aspects of Tai Chi help to lower stress levels and promote a sense of well-being.
4. *Cardiovascular Health*: Can improve cardiovascular fitness and endurance.
5. *Pain Management*: Beneficial for people with chronic conditions such as arthritis by reducing pain and improving quality of life.

Tai Chi Practice:

1. *Forms and Postures*: Tai Chi consists of a series of postures or forms that flow smoothly from one to the next. Each form has specific movements that target different parts of the body.
2. *Consistency*: Regular practice is essential to gain the full benefits. Many people practice Tai Chi daily or several times a week.
3. *Adaptability*: Tai Chi can be adapted to fit individual fitness levels and health conditions, making it accessible to a wide range of people.

Tai Chi is often practiced in groups or through guided sessions with a teacher, but it can also be done alone once the basic forms are learned. Its combination of physical exercise, mindfulness, and relaxation makes it a holistic approach to health and well-being.

Prenatal Massage*:* Treat yourself to a prenatal massage to relieve tension and promote relaxation.

Gentle Stretching*:* Incorporate gentle stretching into your daily routine to maintain flexibility and ease any discomfort.

Conclusion

The Law of Least Effort teaches us to let go of unnecessary struggles and to flow with the natural rhythm of life. By embracing this law, pregnant mothers can create a nurturing and peaceful environment for both themselves and their babies. Remember, the journey of pregnancy is unique and personal. Allow yourself to experience it with ease and joy, knowing that by doing less, you are often achieving more for you and your baby's well-being.

Chapter 5

The Law of Intention and Desire

Setting Positive Intentions for Your Pregnancy and Birth

Pregnancy is a profound journey, not just of physical transformation but of emotional and spiritual growth. As you embark on this journey, setting positive intentions can create a foundation of optimism and empowerment. Intentions are more than wishes; they are powerful declarations of what you aim to achieve and experience.

The Power of Positive Intentions

Positive intentions set a tone of hope and determination. They help align your mind, body, and spirit with the desired outcome of a healthy and joyful pregnancy and birth. As Deepak Chopra eloquently puts it, "Intention is the starting point of every dream—the seed of creation."

Story: A Mother's Affirmation

Consider the story of Maya, a mother who faced several challenges in her first pregnancy. With her second child, Maya decided to approach things differently. Every morning, she spent a few moments setting her intentions. She would say aloud, "I am healthy, my baby is healthy, and I am grateful for this journey." Throughout her pregnancy, she remained focused on these positive affirmations, which helped her navigate the ups and downs with grace and confidence.

Practical Steps for Setting Intentions

1. *Morning Affirmations*: Start each day with a positive affirmation related to your pregnancy. For example, "Today, I nurture myself and my baby with love and care."

2. *Mindful Breathing*: Take deep breaths and visualize your intentions with each inhale, releasing any negativity with each exhale.

3. *Gratitude Journal*: Write down three things you are grateful for every day, reinforcing a positive mindset.

Visualizing a Healthy and Joyful Journey

Visualization is a powerful tool that can help you manifest your desires by creating a mental image of your ideal outcome. By imagining a healthy and joyful pregnancy, you are more likely to experience it.

The Science Behind Visualization

Research has shown that visualization can significantly impact our physical and mental well-being. When you visualize something vividly, your brain processes it as a real experience, triggering the same neural pathways that are activated during the actual experience. This means that positive visualization can enhance your overall pregnancy experience.

Story: Emma's Visualization Practice

Emma was anxious about her upcoming delivery, having heard numerous horror stories from friends and family. Her midwife suggested she practice visualization. Every night before bed, Emma would close her eyes and imagine a peaceful, smooth delivery. She visualized herself holding her healthy baby, feeling calm and joyful. When the day arrived, Emma's delivery was indeed smooth, and she felt a sense of peace throughout the process, attributing much of her calmness to her visualization practice.

Techniques for Effective Visualization

1. *Create a Vision Board*: Gather images and words that represent your ideal pregnancy and birth, and place them on a board where you can see them daily.

2. *Guided Meditation*: Use guided meditation apps or recordings that focus on positive pregnancy and birth experiences.

3. *Daily Visualization:* Spend a few minutes each day visualizing your healthy pregnancy and joyful birth. See yourself in vivid detail, experiencing everything as you desire.

Manifesting Your Desires with Clarity

Manifestation involves bringing your desires into reality through clear intentions, unwavering belief, and aligned actions. When you are clear about what you want, you can take purposeful steps toward achieving it.

The Clarity of Desire

Clarity is essential in the manifestation process. Knowing exactly what you want allows you to focus your energy and actions towards achieving it. "When you want something, all the universe conspires in helping you to achieve it," Paulo Coelho famously wrote in "The Alchemist."

Story: Clara's Birth Plan

Clara had always envisioned a natural birth. She wrote down her birth plan, detailing her preferences and desires. She shared this plan with her healthcare provider and ensured that everyone involved was on the same page. Clara's clarity of desire and proactive communication helped her achieve the birth experience she had always wanted, surrounded by support and understanding.

Steps to Manifest Your Desires

1. Write Down Your Desires: Be specific about what you want for your pregnancy and birth. Write it down in detail.
2. Believe in Your Desires: Cultivate an unwavering belief that you can achieve your desires. Surround yourself with supportive people and positive affirmations.
3. Take Aligned Actions: Make choices and take actions that align with your desires. For instance, if you desire a healthy pregnancy, prioritize nutritious food, regular exercise, and prenatal care.

Quotes to Inspire

"The energy of the mind is the essence of life." – Aristotle

"What you seek is seeking you." – Rumi

Integrating the Law of Intention and Desire into Your Daily Life

Daily Practices

1. *Morning and Evening Rituals*: Begin and end your day with intentions and visualizations. This consistency will reinforce your positive mindset.
2. *Mindfulness and Meditation:* Incorporate mindfulness and meditation into your routine to stay connected with your intentions and desires.

3. *Positive Affirmations*: Use affirmations throughout the day to maintain a positive focus. For example, "I am creating a healthy and joyful pregnancy."

Story: Sarah's Journey

Sarah was a first-time mother who struggled with anxiety. She decided to integrate the Law of Intention and Desire into her pregnancy journey. Every morning, she meditated, visualized her healthy pregnancy, and set her intentions. Throughout the day, she repeated positive affirmations and practiced gratitude. Sarah found that her anxiety diminished, and she felt more in control and at peace. Her birth experience was empowering, and she credited her daily practices for the positive outcome.

Conclusion

The Law of Intention and Desire is a powerful principle that can transform your pregnancy journey. By setting positive intentions, visualizing a healthy and joyful experience, and manifesting your desires with clarity, you can create the pregnancy and birth you dream of. Remember, you have the power within you to shape your reality. Embrace this journey with an open heart and a focused mind, and let the magic unfold.

- "You are the creator of your own reality." – Abraham-Hicks

Chapter 6

The Law of Detachment

Introduction

The journey of pregnancy is filled with a multitude of emotions, from joy and excitement to fear and uncertainty. As expectant mothers, it's natural to have questions and concerns about the unknowns that lie ahead. The Law of Detachment teaches us the power of letting go—of fear, uncertainty, and the need to control every outcome. By embracing this law, we can cultivate a sense of peace and trust in the natural process of pregnancy.

In this chapter, we will explore how the Law of Detachment can transform your pregnancy experience. We will delve into the key aspects of releasing fear and uncertainty, trusting the natural process of pregnancy, and embracing flexibility and adaptability. Through stories, examples, and quotations, you will discover practical ways to implement these principles in your daily life.

Releasing Fear and Uncertainty

Fear and uncertainty are common companions during pregnancy. The "what ifs" can be overwhelming, and the desire to control every detail, can lead to stress and anxiety. The Law of Detachment encourages us to release these fears and uncertainties, allowing us to focus on the present moment.

Story: Anjali's Journey to Letting Go

Anjali, a first-time mother, found herself constantly worried about her baby's health. She read every book, followed every piece of advice, and yet, she couldn't shake off the anxiety. One day, she attended a prenatal yoga class where the instructor introduced the concept of detachment.

The instructor shared a simple exercise: "Close your eyes and imagine placing all your fears and worries into a balloon. Now, let that balloon float away." Anjali practiced this visualization daily, and slowly, she began to feel a sense of relief. She realized that while she couldn't control every outcome, she could control how she responded to her fears.

"As you release the fear of the unknown, you make space for the beauty of the present moment to unfold." – Unknown

Trusting the Natural Process of Pregnancy

Pregnancy is a natural process, and trusting in the wisdom of your body can bring immense comfort. The Law of Detachment teaches us to have faith in the journey, knowing that everything is unfolding as it should.

Example: The Trusting Mother

Consider the story of Maya, who experienced complications in her first trimester. Instead of succumbing to fear, Maya chose to trust in her body's ability to nurture her baby. She focused on staying healthy, meditating, and practicing positive affirmations.

Her mantra was simple: "My body knows what to do. I trust the process." Maya's calm and trusting attitude not only helped her reduce stress but also created a positive environment for her baby. Her faith in the natural process of pregnancy was rewarded with a smooth delivery and a healthy baby.

> *"Trust the process. Your body was designed to create and nurture life. Believe in its innate wisdom." – Deepak Chopra*

Embracing Flexibility and Adaptability

Pregnancy often comes with unexpected changes, and the ability to adapt is crucial. The Law of Detachment encourages us to embrace flexibility, allowing us to flow with the natural rhythms of life.

Story: Rekha's Adaptable Attitude

Rekha, in her second trimester, planned every detail of her pregnancy. However, when she developed gestational diabetes, her carefully crafted plans had to change. Instead of feeling defeated, Rekha embraced the situation with an adaptable mindset.

She learned about gestational diabetes, adjusted her diet, and followed her doctor's advice. Rekha's willingness to adapt not only ensured her health but also taught her the importance of flexibility. She found joy in the unexpected, and her adaptable attitude made her pregnancy journey more fulfilling.

> *"The measure of intelligence is the ability to change." – Albert Einstein*

Practical Tips for Practicing the Law of Detachment During Pregnancy

1. *Daily Meditation*: Spend a few minutes each day in quiet meditation, focusing on letting go of fears and trusting the natural process of pregnancy.

2. *Affirmations*: Create positive affirmations that reinforce trust and detachment. Repeat them throughout the day.

3. *Visualization*: Use visualization techniques to release fears. Imagine placing your worries in a balloon and watching it float away.

4. *Flexible Planning*: While it's good to have plans, be open to changes. Embrace flexibility and trust that everything will unfold as it should.

5. *Connect with Nature:* Spend time in nature to remind yourself of the natural rhythms and processes. Nature's cycles can be a powerful reminder to trust the process.

Conclusion

The Law of Detachment is a powerful tool for pregnant mothers. By releasing fear and uncertainty, trusting the natural process of pregnancy, and embracing flexibility and adaptability, you can create a more peaceful and joyful pregnancy experience. Remember, the journey of pregnancy is unique to each mother, and by practicing detachment, you can navigate this journey with grace and confidence.

As you embrace the Law of Detachment, may you find the strength to let go, the courage to trust, and the wisdom to adapt. Your journey is a beautiful unfolding of life, and by detaching from the need to control every outcome, you allow the natural process to flow with ease.

> *"Detachment is not that you should own nothing, but that nothing should own you." – Ali Ibn Abi Talib*

May your pregnancy journey be filled with peace, trust, and the joy of embracing the unknown.

Chapter 7

The Law of Dharma (Purpose in Life)

Recognizing the Sacred Role of Motherhood

Motherhood is a sacred journey, a profound transformation that aligns a woman with her deepest purpose. This journey is a reflection of the Law of Dharma, which emphasizes living in alignment with one's true nature and fulfilling one's unique purpose. For pregnant mothers, recognizing the sacred role of motherhood can bring a sense of peace and fulfillment.

Story: The Embrace of Motherhood

Meera, a first-time mother, felt overwhelmed by the changes pregnancy brought into her life. She attended a prenatal yoga class where the instructor spoke about the sacred role of motherhood. This perspective shifted Meera's view. She began to see her pregnancy not just as a biological process, but as a spiritual journey.

Embracing her role as a mother, Meera felt a deep connection to her unborn child, and this realization filled her with purpose and joy.

> *"Motherhood: All love begins and ends there." – Robert Browning*

Recognizing the sacred role of motherhood involves understanding that being a mother is not just a duty but a calling. It is a unique opportunity to nurture, guide, and shape a new life, which is both a privilege and a responsibility.

Finding Meaning and Fulfillment in Pregnancy

Pregnancy is a time of immense change, but it also offers a profound opportunity for finding meaning and fulfillment. By embracing the Law of Dharma, a pregnant mother can connect with the deeper significance, of this phase, in her life.

Example: Journaling for Self-Discovery

Priya, another expectant mother, found herself grappling with anxiety about the future. She started a daily journaling practice, where she reflected on her thoughts, dreams, and fears. Through this practice, Priya discovered a deep sense of fulfillment and meaning in her pregnancy. She began to appreciate each moment, finding joy in the small, everyday experiences of carrying her child.

> *"Pregnancy is a process that invites you to surrender to the unseen force behind all life." – Judy Ford*

By consciously engaging in activities that foster self-reflection and mindfulness, such as journaling or meditation, pregnant mothers can uncover the deeper meaning behind their experiences and find fulfillment in the journey of bringing new life into the world.

Connecting with Your Life's Purpose as a Mother

The Law of Dharma teaches that every individual has a unique purpose in life. For pregnant women, this law can be a guide to connect with their life's purpose as mothers. This connection can bring clarity, motivation, and a profound sense of direction.

Story: The Path of Purpose

Anjali always believed that her purpose was to excel in her career. When she became pregnant, she struggled with the fear of losing her professional identity. A mentor suggested she explore her dharma in the context of motherhood. Anjali took a step back and reflected on how her nurturing qualities, leadership skills, and passion for growth could translate into her role as a mother. She realized that her purpose now included raising a child who could also make a positive impact on the world.

> *"There is no role in life more essential and more eternal than that of motherhood." – M. Russell Ballard*

Connecting with one's life purpose as a mother involves recognizing the skills, passions, and values that define you and understanding how they can be applied to motherhood. It is about seeing the continuity in your life's journey and embracing the new dimension that motherhood brings to your purpose.

Practical Steps for Pregnant Mothers to Implement the Law of Dharma

1. Meditation and Mindfulness:

Engage in regular meditation to quiet the mind and connect with your inner self. Mindfulness practices can help you stay present and appreciate the journey of pregnancy.

2. Journaling:

Reflect on your experiences, thoughts, and feelings through journaling. This practice can help you uncover deeper insights about your purpose and find meaning in your daily experiences.

3. Seek Support and Guidance:
Surround yourself with supportive individuals who understand and respect your journey. Mentors, friends, or support groups can provide valuable perspectives and encouragement.

4. Embrace Your Unique Qualities:
Recognize and celebrate the unique qualities that you bring to motherhood. Reflect on how your strengths and passions can enhance your role as a mother.

5. Stay Connected to Your Values:
Keep your core values at the forefront of your journey. They will guide your decisions and help you stay aligned with your purpose as you navigate the challenges and joys of pregnancy and motherhood.

Example: A Community of Mothers

A local community center offered a program called "Mothers Connecting with Purpose." It brought together pregnant women to share their stories, support each other, and explore their unique paths. This community helped each mother feel validated in her experiences and empowered in her journey, fostering a strong sense of purpose and connection.

"Motherhood is the exquisite inconvenience of being another person's everything." – Unknown

By incorporating the Law of Dharma into their lives, pregnant mothers can transform their experience from one of mere survival to one of profound growth and fulfillment. Understanding and embracing their sacred role, finding meaning in their journey, and connecting with their life's purpose, as mothers can lead to a more joyful and empowered experience of pregnancy.

Chapter 8

Practical Applications of the Seven Spiritual Laws of Success During Pregnancy

Pregnancy is a time of profound transformation and growth. By integrating the Seven Spiritual Laws of Success into daily life, expectant mothers can cultivate a sense of peace, purpose, and fulfillment. This chapter will explore practical ways to apply these laws, create a supportive environment, and build a community of love and support during this special time.

Daily Practices to Integrate the Seven Laws

1. The Law of Pure Potentiality: Embracing Inner Self

Practice: Start each day with a few minutes of meditation or mindfulness. This practice can help connect with your inner self and embrace the pure potentiality within you.

Example: Priya, a soon-to-be mother, set aside 10 minutes each morning to sit quietly and focus on her breathing. This simple practice helped her stay centered and connected with her baby, allowing her to approach her day with calmness and clarity.

"The greatest achievement was at first and for a time a dream." — James Allen

2. The Law of Giving and Receiving: Cultivating Generosity

Practice: Engage in small acts of kindness each day. Whether it's helping a neighbor or volunteering at a local charity, these acts can create a positive flow of energy and reinforce a sense of connection.

Example: Aisha volunteered at a community center for expectant mothers, sharing her experiences and providing support. Her involvement not only helped others but also deepened her own sense of fulfillment and connection.

"The best way to find yourself is to lose yourself in the service of others." — Mahatma Gandhi

3. The Law of Karma: Creating Positive Outcomes

Practice: Reflect on your actions and intentions. Strive to make choices that align with your values and contribute positively to your well-being and that of your baby.

Example: When Maya faced stressful situations, she reminded herself to respond with patience and kindness. By choosing positive reactions, she noticed a reduction in stress and an improved atmosphere at home.

"You reap what you sow." — The Bible

4. The Law of Least Effort: Letting Go of Stress

Practice: Practice gentle movement and relaxation techniques, such as prenatal yoga or deep breathing exercises, to release tension and embrace a more relaxed approach to challenges.

Example: Sita incorporated prenatal yoga into her daily routine, which helped her manage stress and maintain a sense of calm. She found that this practice also contributed to her overall physical well-being during pregnancy.

> *"In the midst of movement and chaos, keep stillness inside of you." — Deepak Chopra*

5. The Law of Intention and Desire: Setting Positive Goals

Practice: Write down your intentions and desires for your pregnancy and childbirth. Visualize these goals regularly to keep your focus and motivation aligned.

Example: Neha created a vision board with images and affirmations related to her ideal birth experience. This visual representation helped her stay focused on her goals and maintained a positive outlook.

> *"The future belongs to those who believe in the beauty of their dreams." — Eleanor Roosevelt*

6. The Law of Detachment: Embracing Flexibility

Practice: Learn to let go of rigid expectations and be open to unexpected changes. Embrace flexibility and adaptability as you navigate the journey of pregnancy.

Example: When Anu's birth plan had to be adjusted due to unforeseen circumstances, she remained open and adaptable. Her ability to let go of control, allowed her to approach the situation with calm and acceptance.

> *"The more we let go, the more we find that what we truly need is right there." — Anonymous*

7. The Law of Dharma (Purpose in Life): Finding Meaning

Practice: Reflect on the sacred role of motherhood and find ways to connect with your deeper purpose. Engage in activities that bring you joy and fulfillment as a mother.

Example: Rina spent time journaling about her experiences and aspirations as a mother. This reflective practice helped her appreciate the significance of her role and provided a deeper sense of purpose.

"Motherhood: All love begins and ends there." — Robert Browning

Creating a Supportive Environment

Creating a nurturing environment is essential for a positive pregnancy experience. Surround yourself with supportive elements that contribute to your well-being:

Create a Comforting Space: Design a calming and comforting environment in your home where you can relax and connect with your baby. Incorporate soothing colors, soft fabrics, and peaceful elements.

Healthy Habits: Establish routines that support your physical and emotional health, such as balanced nutrition, regular exercise, and adequate rest.

Positive Influences: Engage with positive, supportive people who uplift and encourage you. Limit exposure to negative or stressful influences.

Building a Community of Love and Support

A strong support network can make a significant difference during pregnancy:

Family and Friends: Reach out to loved ones for emotional and practical support. Share your experiences and lean on them for encouragement.

Support Groups: Join prenatal or parenting groups to connect with other expectant mothers. These groups provide a platform for sharing experiences, advice, and support.

Professional Guidance: Seek advice from healthcare professionals, such as midwives, doulas, or therapists, to support your physical and emotional needs.

By integrating these practices and fostering a supportive environment, expectant mothers can navigate their pregnancy with greater ease and fulfillment. Embrace the journey with an open heart and mind, and remember that every step taken with intention and love contributes to a beautiful and transformative experience.

> *"It is not the strongest of the species that survive, nor the most intelligent, but the one most responsive to change." — Charles Darwin*

Conclusion

Reflecting on Your Journey

As you reach the conclusion of this spiritual journey through pregnancy, take a moment to reflect on the path you've traveled. Each of the Seven Spiritual Laws has offered you a unique perspective and set of practices to enrich your experience as an expecting mother. You've learned to connect with your inner self, to give and receive love freely, to make conscious choices, and to embrace the flow of life with ease and grace.

Preparing for the Transition to Motherhood

The transition from pregnancy to motherhood is a profound and transformative experience. As you prepare for this new chapter, remember the wisdom you've gained from the Seven Spiritual Laws:

Pure Potentiality: Stay connected with your inner peace and infinite possibilities. Trust that you have all the potential within you to be a wonderful mother.

Giving: Continue to nurture and give love, both to your baby and to yourself. Small acts of kindness will create a ripple effect of positivity.

Karma: Be mindful of your actions and their impact. Your loving intentions will shape the future in beautiful ways.

Least Effort: Embrace the natural flow of motherhood. Let go of perfectionism and allow things to unfold naturally.

Intention and Desire: Hold a clear vision of the kind of mother you want to be. Your intentions will guide your actions and help you manifest your desires.

Detachment: Release fears and anxieties. Trust in the process and be flexible with the unexpected changes that come with motherhood.

Dharma: Embrace your purpose as a mother. This role is sacred and uniquely yours, filled with opportunities for love and growth.

Embracing the Future with Confidence and Joy

The journey ahead is filled with unknown, but it is also brimming with joy, love, and discovery. Embrace each moment with an open heart and a confident spirit. Trust in yourself, in your body, and in the bond, you are building with your baby. Know that you are supported by the universe, and that everything you need is within you.

Remember that you are not alone on this journey. Seek out and cherish the support of your partner, family, friends, and community. Share your experiences, your joys, and your challenges. In doing so, you create a web of support and love that will sustain you through the beautiful adventure of motherhood.

As you approach the culmination of your pregnancy journey, it's essential to take a moment to reflect on the incredible path you've traveled. This period of transformation has been filled with unique experiences, challenges, and triumphs that have shaped you into the mother you are becoming. Reflecting on this journey allows you to appreciate your growth and the profound connection you've built with your baby.

Preparing for the transition to motherhood involves embracing the changes and anticipating the new responsibilities that await. Equip yourself with knowledge and resources to ease the transition, such as understanding newborn care, seeking support from loved ones, and nurturing your well-being. Preparing both mentally and physically will help you navigate the early days of motherhood with greater ease and confidence.

Carry forward the strength, patience, and wisdom you've gained, and approach each day with an open heart and a positive outlook.

By reflecting on your journey, preparing diligently, and embracing the future with confidence, you will be well-equipped to fully enjoy the experience of motherhood. This knowledge will not only support you during pregnancy but will also empower you as you step into this beautiful, transformative role.

Final Thoughts

As you close this book and step forward into motherhood, carry with you the essence of the Seven Spiritual Laws. Let them be a source of strength, wisdom, and inspiration. Your journey is unique and beautiful, and you are more than capable of navigating it with grace and love.

Thank you for allowing this book to be a part of your pregnancy journey. May you and your baby be blessed with health, happiness, and a deep sense of connection.

With love and blessings,

[DR MEHUL KIRITKUMAR NAYAK]

MASTERING THE 7 SPIRITUAL LAWS OF SUCCESS IN PREGNANCY

Too many of us grew up with the belief that achieving success requires relentless hard work, grim determination, and intense ambition. As a result, we may have struggled for years and even reached some of our goals, but wound up, feeling exhausted, our lives out of balance.

In "The Divine Path to Motherhood: Seven Spiritual Laws for a Blissful Pregnancy" Dr. Mehul Kiritkumar Nayak reveals that such desperate striving isn't necessary or even desirable. In the natural world, creation comes forth with ease. A seed doesn't struggle to become a tree—it simply unfolds in grace. The Seven Spiritual Laws of success during pregnancy are powerful principles; put into practice they set you on a direct course to authentically achieve your goals.

The laws of success are easy to understand and apply. Use these daily steps to incorporate The Seven Spiritual Laws during pregnancy journey:

Sunday: The Law of Pure Potentiality

During pregnancy, embracing silence and simply being present can be profoundly beneficial. Dedicate time to meditate for 30 minutes twice a day, focusing on the new life growing within you. Silently observe and connect with the innate intelligence of your developing baby. Practice non-judgment towards yourself and others, fostering a calm and nurturing environment for both you and your child. This mindfulness can help you stay centered and in tune with your body and your baby's needs.

Monday: The Law of Giving

During pregnancy, the practice of giving and receiving can create a nurturing and supportive atmosphere. Today, offer a kind word or a small token of appreciation to those you meet, such as a compliment or a flower. Embrace the gifts you receive, whether they are physical items, support, or love. Keep the flow of positive energy by sharing care, affection, appreciation, and love with those around you. This exchange fosters a loving environment that benefits both you and your baby, promoting emotional well-being and connection.

Tuesday: The Law of Karma

During pregnancy, your actions and thoughts hold significant influence over your well-being and that of your baby. Each positive action you take, generates a force of energy that nurtures both you and your child. Choose actions that spread happiness and positivity for those around you, such as helping others, sharing kind words, or simply being present. This ensures that happiness and success flow back to you, creating a harmonious and supportive environment for your pregnancy journey. By fostering positive energy, you enhance your own sense of well-being and contribute to the healthy development of your baby.

Wednesday: The Law of Least Effort

During pregnancy, embracing acceptance and simplicity can greatly enhance your experience. Accept people, situations, and events as they unfold, acknowledging that each moment is part of your unique journey. Take responsibility for your health and well-being, and view challenges as opportunities for growth, rather than problems. Let go of the need to defend your choices or point of view; trust that you are making the best decisions for you and your baby. By practicing acceptance and minimizing resistance, you create a peaceful and supportive environment, reducing stress and promoting a positive pregnancy experience.

Thursday: The Law of Intention and Desire

During pregnancy, your intentions and desires can shape your experience and the bond with your baby. Write down your hopes and aspirations for your pregnancy, childbirth, and motherhood. Trust that each intention you set carries the potential for fulfillment. If things don't go as planned, have faith that there is a reason, perhaps guiding you to a better outcome. By focusing on positive intentions and remaining open to the journey, you nurture a positive mindset, supporting both your well-being and your baby's development.

Friday: The Law of Detachment

During pregnancy, embracing the Law of Detachment can bring peace and flexibility. Allow yourself and your baby the freedom to grow and develop naturally, without imposing rigid expectations. Avoid forcing solutions to challenges; instead, trust that answers and resolutions will emerge in their own time. Embrace the uncertainty of pregnancy as a journey towards freedom, understanding that it's a natural part of this transformative experience. By letting go of control, you create a supportive and stress-free environment for both you and your baby, fostering healthy development and well-being.

Saturday: The Law of Dharma

During pregnancy, seek to connect with your higher Self and discover your unique talents. Reflect on how these abilities can serve your growing family and community. Embrace your role as a mother, using your strengths to nurture and support your baby and loved ones. By aligning with your purpose and serving others with your unique gifts, you create a fulfilling and abundant experience, bringing joy and bliss to your pregnancy journey and beyond. This sense of purpose not only enhances your well-being but also creates a positive environment for your baby's development.

www.ingramcontent.com/pod-product-compliance
Lightning Source LLC
LaVergne TN
LVHW041637070526
838199LV00052B/3405